Dialogue with a Dead Man

For Jann + Tom,
I hope you find
something here to
like!

9.26.74   Jim

DIALOGUE
WITH A DEAD MAN

Jim Miller

University of Georgia Press, Athens

Acknowledgments

The author and the publisher gratefully acknowledge permission to reprint these poems which originally appeared in the publications here noted: "Old Man All My Life," *American Weave;* "Crossing" and "Driving to the Gulf," *Appalachian Harvest;* "Stranger," "Remembering Aunt Vi" and "Family Reunion," *Approaches;* "Miss Hattie Mae, Aged 92, Dies at the Quality Extended Care Facility," *College Heights Herald;* "County Seat" and "Home Movie," *Green River Review;* "Meeting," *Kentucky Folklore Record;* "On Native Ground," "Berry Picking," and "A Mountain Field," *Mountain Life & Work;* "Old Ghost" and "Stalking," *North Carolina Folklore;* "Squirrel Stand," *Pegasus;* "Cut-Over Woods," *Penny Poems From Midwestern University;* "Trellis," *Plume & Sword;* "Remembering Wade Robinson" and "A Soldier," *Poems From the Hills* (Copyright 1972 by MHC Publications); "Martin Gets Away," *south;* "Writing My Name" and "The Bee Woman," *Southern Poetry Review.*

The following poems appeared in *Copperhead Cane* (Copyright 1964 by Robert Moore Allen): "Copperhead Cane," "For S. F. S.," "The Grave," "The Reverend Mr. Thick," "Hanlon Mountain in Mist," "Closing the House," "Still More to Disbelieve," "Hanging Burley," "After the Hunt," "Winter Hunt," "Burning Tobacco Beds," "Fencepost," "Horse Knob," "Coming off the Lake," "Hound and Hook," "In a Mountain Pasture," "A Friend," and "Visit to an Ancient Lady."

Contents

PART THREE: *Family Reunion*

PART ONE: *COPPERHEAD CANE*

Copperhead Cane

Craft carving with fancy on the plain
held in the hand of sleight
knows how to shape
the seasoned stock of need to grave delight.

Often I've seen you make,
by carving a needful sourwood walking stick,
a spiraling snake.

Wrought out of my gnarled grief by that same trick,
these poems are a copperhead cane.

For S. F. S.

Graveward to this green tent I too came burdened,
though other hands than mine, yet none more willing,
waited to man the metal grips, to bear
you briefly through this rain up Newfound Hill.
Walking beside the water-beaded coffin,
I saw how feet, schooled in these hills at yours,
climbed on the rutted clay; where others slipped,
they did not even soil their Sunday shoes.

In Doggett's Gap, by Double Springs where we
made camp, we knew another tent, another
time, squirrel-time in the Bear Wallow,
and rain rolled from our blue-barreled rifles.
Climbing the hill head-down behind you, I marked
how wisely your feet held, fast on the slippery rocks.

The Grave

Now comes the darkest, longest night of all,
the first night in the grave. The new-made mound
is hill beneath a tent-sky, the world a click
of stone on stone heard breathless underground.
Dawn: the tent comes down. Footfalls faintly
heard, as if the ear were to the ground.
Now nights are moments when a cloud drifts past
the sun, days earth-cracks on the mound.
Summers bake, autumns brown and burn,
winters break and crumble, split the ground.
In distant silent springs cloud-shadows fly,
earth-cracks creep across the settled mound.
Cloud-shadows fly, cracks creep across the mound,
till shadows fly, cracks creep on level ground.

The Reverend Mr. Thick

Commissioned to preach your funeral, the Reverend Mr. Thick,
the one you thought a fool, not looking thinner,
rejoiced in God's great bounty, your daughter's dinner.
He ate, unless I mistake my arithmetic,
four golden drumsticks in quick succession,
three wings, two necks, a gizzard, rolls untold,
then started a story (already we felt consoled),
but had to break it off in a long digression.

Leaning on the lectern, mating trite trope to trope,
backed by the dollars and cents on Sunday's roll,
he plunged us into doubt about your soul;
then when the women wept, he gave us hope.
Just as in life, the calmest man about,
you were the least concerned, the least in doubt.

Hanlon Mountain in Mist

Ril Sams came by, but now the house is still
and cold with dread. Unless this weather breaks,
I look for another grave on Newfound Hill.
Rain rumbles on the roof, splashes from the eaves,
and foams and bubbles into tubs below
the spouts. The barn, the shingles on the crib
drip black with rain. Springhouse mosses grow
frog-green and Hanlon's top is lost in mist.
Ril Sams climbed Hanlon with his hounds last night,
but when they winded something below the top,
and wouldn't go beyond the lantern light,
and trembled on the lead, then he came home.
I trust the hounds: they know what made them stop,
what waits there in the mist on Hanlon's top.

Closing the House

While rumbling trunks pushed down the hall upstairs
boom like the scudding thunderstorm just passed,
we bear out cardboard boxes, tables, and chairs
stripped from rooms grown hollow, strange and vast.
We plod, as humdrum over such a deep
as veteran thieves lifting petty loot,
too dried-sweat stiff to feel the sweep
of grief that rolls the floor from underfoot.
Mule-footed plundering done, the rooms all sacked,
now only the furrowed shell that stops the door
remains, impounding the roaring foaming fact
all the years. I pick it off the floor.
It murmurs in my ear, floods my breath,
and drowns me in the sea-sound of your death.

Still More to Disbelieve

Still more to disbelieve: the spruce is gone.
When broomsage grew above my head here where
the water shoots, it seemed to me a lone
old bearded fisherman dangling its own bare
roots for lines. Although we saw the creek,
just days before you died, run red and swell
and snaillike leave a track of slime, this streak
of sun is strange to see where shadow fell.

So much dike-work to do, both in and out:
I'll stand knee-deep, feeling the icy rush,
sand swept from underfoot, and sink stout
stakes. Chilled and shivering, I'll throw in brush.

At night, my grief a traveled, polished stone,
I'll pass and disbelieve I hunt alone.

Hanging Burley

I'm straddling the top tier, my wet shirt clinging;
under this hot tin roof sweat balls and rolls.
Smothered in gummy green, my seared eyes stinging,
I'm hanging burley tobacco on peeled tier poles.
A funeral mood below me on the ground:
a blank-faced filing past the loaded sled;
a coming with a solemn, swishing sound;
tobacco borne as if it were the dead.
Even the children, shadowed by our grief,
hang broken leaves and ape the studied pace.
—Let burley come, and save each frog-eyed leaf,
till every wilted stick is hung in place,
till gazing on the naked, empty field,
we see, row after row, your death revealed.

After the Hunt

Catch up the hounds by collar and scruff
and drop the cattle gate!
The fox has holed in Reynolds Bluff,
the moon is low, it's late.
    He savors flame and crowds the fire,
    a stubborn leaf in frosty air,
    the wrinkled brown old hunter.

The truck's hood skims the safety rail
and veering, blunt and black,
dogs a darting cottontail,
a hound's nose on the track.
    He nods and pitches when I brake,
    a leaf that falls when branches shake,
    the wrinkled brown old hunter.

The truck hums down to Turkey Creek,
loose boards slap on the bridge.
The sun comes up, a first red streak,
through white oaks on the ridge.
    He sleeps beside me on the seat,
    dry leaf in morning's surge and heat,
    the wrinkled brown old hunter.

Winter Hunt

Forgetful by the fire that I'm alone,
I almost told a ticking pin oak leaf
the hounds have lost the fox by Turkey Creek.
Scattered from bottom to bluff, they're howling now,
and still I crouch, and shivering crowd the flames,
still slow to leave this knob and stumble home
on cracking, ice-caked cattle tracks.
And as I savor fire in frost and cold,
I feel you hovering like a frozen breath;
you tremble too and cherish tended warmth,
numbed by a night where stones sweat crystal-crust.
Abandoned there, first frantic like the leaf,
then still, you'd hear the scraggly frost-hounds
come padding, snarling, padding on the rime.

Old Man All My Life

You labored nights throwing fodder down
from the loft into the pine pole racks,
to cattle stumbling on their frozen tracks,
then woke to dream the thin and soundless town.
After she found you walking on the frost,
saying you'd just stepped out to feed your stock,
you'd wake your daughter fumbling at the lock.
Dreamer on sleet-rattled leaves, you crossed
a crust of rime, then woke to the innocent snow
falling now in the subdivision of stones
on Newfound Hill. You don't know
how slyly days and nights in town foretold
this thin and soundless dream away from home.
You fumble at the lock, confused and cold.

Burning Tobacco Beds

I'm burning tobacco beds alone tonight
and talking to myself and to the flames.
October I chopped a clearing on this ridge,
piled high the brush, weighted it down with chunks.
No weedseed will be left among these ashes;
before the dogwoods blossom on these hills,
misty tobacco beds will patch the slopes
like caterpillar nests in apple trees.

I just sat down and leaned against this stump,
and fired my pipe and looked up at the moon.
A chunk fell down and sparks flew up like quail.
So used to burning tobacco beds with you,
I turned and thought I saw you through the smoke,
working like that old brush-piler on the moon.

Fencepost

Mending the fence we built one fall together,
I come to the spring below the mountain field.
This stake here by the spring drain needs no bracing;
it's sprouted now (you left the post unpeeled)
and feels so firm, so solid in the ground,
I'd say it's taken root.—Death's sickle-sweep
is wide:—bone-man on the branchbank,
in denims and an old black hat, still half-asleep
at foggy dawn, I've heard him giving his blade
a whetstone's lick and promise by the spill.
But death would have to be a newground
grubber, and dig out every root, and still
he'd not be sure roots wouldn't send down roots,
or sure that stubble wouldn't send up shoots.

Horse Knob

Horse Knob's the sawbrier cemetery
now of foxy nights we lay by fires
and heard the hounds. I ripped through elderberry
bushes, beggar's-lice and sawblade briers,
and climbed on copper scalds baked in waves
of heat. Winded, I stopped beside the fence.
It was like hunting up forgotten graves
on Newfound Hill, where monuments
are overgrown. I searched about for signs
of our fires: a settled, rain-packed hill
of ashes in tall grass. Off in the pines:
rainwater and green slime in a terrapin shell.
A crow cawed brazenly. The dry fly's drone
was time before red clay formed flesh and bone.

Coming Off the Lake

Mounting, dipping—bobbing fishing float
riding rolling green—the speeding land,
a piney point, runs lapping at my boat
till point and prow collide in grass and sand.
Persuaded long by glassy undulation,
I jolt the ground and stagger, ripple-kneed,
heaved, buoyed on green grief's imitation,
washed past swimming tree and wavering weed.

About my drifting boat enameled trees
on well-turned hills, and my own fired-clay face,
broken to painted bits by every breeze,
went rippling off, cracked ruins of time and space.
In gloom below the promenading waves
lay sad dark logs like underwater graves.

Hound and Hook

Drawn by the hounds, whining to go fox-free,
we climbed Horse Knob a frog-town Saturday night
and heard the race from a ring of lantern light.
At dawn the fox leaped crimson over trees.

By the bobbing hissing lanterns we could see
our slanting lines swim at the shore of night
and water smoke in the creaking ring of light.
At dawn a fish leaped silver over trees.

With five eager hounds straining on the lead,
I walk by lantern light on foxy nights.
Or look for me in a rocking ring of light
when water smokes and dawn leaps over trees.

With hound and hook I hunt and fish the night
your shadow stepped into beyond this light.

In a Mountain Pasture

Endings have a wile, a mountain cunning,
and only seem to sleep, like groundhogs sunning
on rocks. We came one morning to mow, not knowing
another walked with a scythe, who left no track,
who made no sign to say, "This is an ending."
There was only the murmur of bees and cattle blowing
their breath on murmuring grass. But crouching, blending
with mottled shade: a secret with its ears laid back.
Dry and brown by the sigh of grazing cattle,
sun-curled leaves in the underbrush,
endings are mountain grouse, feathered things
that beating up through berry briers, startle
the heart, confound it with a whirring rush
of leaping thrashing leaves and limbs and wings.
Above me on the ridge a brazen crow
stares from the standing bones of a chestnut tree.
Why is he watching me?
What does he know?

PART TWO: *DIALOGUE WITH A DEAD MAN*

Walking,

walking through March-brown fields
in feeble sun,
following trails
you made from house to barn,
from barn to cattle-gap
my shadow moving, moving
with bunched black shadows of whitesheep
roving.
Ricked cane rattles in March wind blowing
over fields where trails you made in winter
are growing
fainter.
Wherever I stop
the fieldstone wall is cold under my hand.
Shadows of whitesheep
fly like faces over the ground.

Old Ghost .

The hounds are growing restless on their tethers.
As light goes out of the cove,
smoke hangs over
the house, the way smoke hangs before bad weather.
Even my gangly, half-grown pup
pacing the lot winds
the red fox making his evening rounds.
Early this morning by the cattle gap
I saw his tracks, round and the size of a quarter,
in soft red clay.
There where the shattered sky
floated in cattle tracks full of water,
I trailed you through pieces of a dream
I was still waking from.

Stalking

And walking in the woods I hear your tread
behind me in the leaves,
while far out ahead,
like skittish grouse in brushy coves,
you're always whirring
out of hearing.

In underwater windrows, drifted streaks
of last year's fallen leaves,
you are the trout that strikes
and quickly moves.
I see only rings
widening.

Meeting

My shadow was my partner in the row.
He was working the slick-handled shadow of his hoe
when out of the patch toward noon there came the sound
of steel on steel two inches underground,—
as if our hoes had hooked each other on that spot.
My shadow's hoe must be of steel, I thought.
And where my chopping hoe came down and struck,
memory rushed like water out of rock.
"When two strike hoes," I said, "it's always sign
they'll work the patch together again sometime.
An old man told me that the last time ever
we worked this patch and our hoes rang together."
Delving there with my hoe, I half-uncovered
a plowpoint, worn and rusted over.
"The man I hoed with last lies under earth,
his plowpoint and his saying of equal worth."
My shadow, standing by me in the row,
waited, and while I rested, raised his hoe.

Dog's Eye

Shaking his ears and stretching, my dog comes
from sleeping in the shed to lick my hand.
The short hairs on his neck begin to stand;
black lips curl from meat-red gums,
from hooked fangs. He growls, stiffens, and shies
away. My face reflected in his eyes
hangs smoky on a papered wall at home,
a dead man's picture in its oval frame.

I can't recall when I was last alone.
You go by day unseen among the living
whose life went out with stars as day came on
and reappears, a star, as light is leaving.
Why have you followed me through this unbroken
round of days and night and never spoken?

Listening

I couldn't wedge a word into your grieving,
not as long as you whispered rhymes down dark
holes in the earth to a face you thought you saw
looking up with dead eyes from the ground.
I could have made two crops from seed to shock,
I could have worn out two good walking sticks
while you talked to a scarecrow of a man,
groaning to every ticking pin oak leaf
the hunt was over. I couldn't speak, not
till you left off talking to your face in black
stumpwater—and talked to me! I wouldn't answer!
For I'm not in the ground, nor the sky either.
I am a live man walking with you,
wanting to throw a shadow into life.

Vine

I am not anything apart from you.
Except as you see, speak, and do,
I have no voice, no hand, or eye.
I have to lie
lodged in you by my own word and deed,
myself inside my seed,
damp in the dark ground of your word,
your life the crack of light I grow toward,
a vine with sick white leaves
unfolding in the cellar of your grief.
I'd just as lief
you left off making pictures of your grief
early and late
and hanging them between me and the light.

Trellis

For my life was heat of the sun, strain, and sweat
of man and mule mingled in newground.
The grating plowpoint darted from root
to stump to rock, snapping singletrees
and tracechains mended in a woodlot
where hens with wilted wings bathed in the chips
and speckled guineas pottericked among
stacked chimneys of stovewood drying.

—Now sloe-eyed cattle are swishing flies
in black shade where you left saplings standing.
Bees pasturing honeysuckle are rising
and drifting down at the springdrain trickle.
Your life is a trellis I train verses up,
just as these roses climb the weathered porch.

Breaking Ground

I break
these poems
like mountain
newgrounds, odd-
shaped fields and
patches cleared from
stump and root-riddled roughs.
Drawing a verse as straight as
any furrow you ever turned from
woods' edge to woods' edge, I'm apt
to remember how you came early on the
sledroad and worked alone to the clack of
singletree, the tracechain's tinkle, a dry fly
thrumming in morning sun. When I've
roughed out the poem and it stands like a wedge of new-
ground driven into woods, I leave it, just as you left fields
and patches—for women and children to cultivate.

Squirrel Stand

Now burley's curing in the high-tiered barn
and yellow leaves ride out on slow black water.
Cold wind moving in the rows of corn
rattles the blades like an old man pulling fodder.
Down from the mountain pastures overnight,
cattle stand by the yellow salt block bawling.
Now it's September in the world; fine rain is falling.

—When gray squirrels had grown fat on hickory nuts,
my gun in the crook of my arm, once I went stepping
through yellow leaves and fine rain falling.
Resting on a ridge above our tents,
I heard what raincrows off in the midst were calling:
my days were growing full, sliding, dropping
like waterbeads along the barbed-wire fence.

Cut-Over Woods

—Hunting brown pheasants in the coves, I remember
you logged here once, a stout man cutting timber.
I hear your axes on the rock-backed ridges
chopping, I hear the singing of your saws,
your hammers ringing driving grabs and wedges,
loggers calling gee and haw and whoa.

—Early along the flinty logging roads,
our frozen breath floating on frosty air,
we came with axes and saws, horses and steers,
fell into gangs and struck off through the woods.
Big oaks that jumped, cracking off their stumps,
we snaked down deep, steep-sided hollows,
riding down ironwoods and willows
in clearings where quick branches slowed to swamps.

—Would you be glad to rest, and looking up
from driving a slippery sourwood glut,
see a white oak tremble in its top,
feel it shake the ground under your feet
braced on the slope?

Shadow-Man

      —Gladder if I could smell,
flat on my stomach at a spring to drink,
green sawdust and crushed pennyrile,
or run my hand along my horse's flank.
Why do you think I haunt you day and night,
hovering always like a frozen breath
in darkness just beyond the lantern light?
The ground buckled under my feet, I fell
like frozen wasps a frosty morning dropping
from high-tiered barns I used to climb.
Now shadow of a man is all I am.

A Hand

A man whose hand was cut off years before
told me once he could feel the hand still moving
and working like a ghost beyond the stump,
claimed it remembered still how a smooth ax
handle felt, and what it was like to crumble
warm earth between the fingers, or drifting
in a boat, to let the fingers trail
through water. And sometimes, before he thought,
the stump would reach out for a hammer or some
such tool, the gone hand grasping for it.
All my life I labored with my hands.
When death like a whirling blade cut me off,
my life became a ghost-hand haunting you,
the body that living on remembers it.

Leaving Home

I recollect you slipped off once and came
to where I plowed knee-high corn among
gray chestnut stumps below Horse Knob.

—I remember crossing a lizardy land
of stone walls and snaky rock piles barefoot.
I passed a bone-white terrapin shell
on a rock, a shiny bottle on a slender
pole, a kind of scarecrow, and a cross wearing
your shirt and old black hat. And I came on
a copperhead you'd killed the day before,
its white belly sun-up atop a wall.
A jarfly rattled and the air coiled
around me—then I heard you calling gee
and haw, the plow's feet scraping rock.
That was the first time ever I followed you
and left behind ground I felt at home on.

A Dark Place

—This time I do believe you mean to follow
me into death and find me plowing a gray
newground of marble tombstones.

—I've followed you so far down into death
I'll never find my way back to home ground.
Once I turned, at the place of bones and coiled
air rattling, looked back and saw the world
with a dead man's eyes. It was like stepping
out of a dazzling noon into a black
barn: all of a sudden blind, I breathed
old air. I stumbled on. My eyes, grown used
to dark, discovered silent shapes of the dead
standing like horses in their sunless stalls.

Night Storms

Since I've looked on the world with a dead man's eyes,
I've been no good for any job of work.
I doubt you are a live man walking with me.
You are the sudden weathers I endure,—
the nightstorms booming on the mind's
headwaters; the lightning licking black
a tree of fear that stands up in the dark;
the hot wind blowing; recollections washing
down like trees uprooted in a flash flood.
And in the morning when the leafy mind
stands dripping, it's you stirring there blows
down another cold shower of remembering.

The Hungry Dead

I think the dead lie hungry in the dark,
below the living teeming in the light.
I've fished nights in a graveyard cove
of drowned trees, my jonboat tethered
to topmost limbs, dead fingers still
reaching up. In the yellow ring of rocking
lantern light minnows swarmed, turning
like silver undersides of willow leaves.
Moving from dark slips between drowned
limbs, crossing deepest shafts of quivering
light, rising, slow black shadows gulped
small fish and fell, shadows into the dark,
just as the hungry dead, rising to light,
devour the living and sink back again.

Last Words

—Well, neither of us will ever be at rest
until our separate voices speak as one
and I move with you, black shadow in sun,
only as you move. You'd do well to remember,
I lost my hold on life but still crave earth.
To me you stand like green-barked second-growth
sprung from stumps and treelaps of old timber.

The Crossing

Always the same dream toward morning and welcome:
we are going, the old man and I,
a gravel road together and glad, a road
that runs through seasons, turning with a creek
between steep-sided hills—going
where two creeks flow together in a flat;
elderbushes drowned in spring floodwaters
stand yellowing, buzzards circle muzzles
of cattle standing knee-deep in blue sky.

I see our shadows walking on cloudbanks
past rotting slabs, a weathered sawdust pile,
past sumac, sassafrass, and dogwoods turning.

An empty house, gray as a hornet's nest,
a sunken shingle roof, a weedy orchard.
Night overtakes us there where sheepnose
apples fall through frosty dark to morning.
As daylight starts to rattle through the woods,
I see us beach a boat across the river.
Pale back of river mist, and grinning,
the sun hangs over white-barked sycamores,
standing bones beside the slipping river.

Our boat half up the bank bobs in the water,
I wake with the taste of copper on my tongue.

A Friend

Under the bluff by Newfound Creek, forever
wavering, still I knew he was roving,
haunting Round Bottom, a wandering holdover,
the unshackled shadow of my Indian interval,
off to my left, dim in his myth, moving
like shadows of thunderheads over the ground,
overalled arrowhead hunter, sunburnt, small.
He was clearly someone other than I, and yet
not hard for me to know, for when I found
black arrowheads, I fancied how he fancied that.
He was clearly someone other than I, and still
I never was sure who saw it first. Was it he
who glimpsed it, half-buried like a turtle shell,
or did I sight that fired-clay Cherokee
vase? I know I yelled no Indian yell.
Relic there among relics, he would not range
from under the bluff. Forked limbs of lightning
cracked in the sky. Turning against a gust,
by willows paling, black sky brightening,
I ran Round Bottom. Big rain splotched the dust
and smacked my face. But he wouldn't leave that place
and follow, running off to the side. It was strange,
abruptly alone, arrowheads clicking in the vase.

Stranger

One day you tramp fields of withered feeling
where long grass lies blown in one direction
and rusty leaves are falling
all the way home.
You turn the light on in a stranger's room
and restlessness like wind in leaves stirs
the dark ground of boredom.
You clean a stranger's desk, throw out his papers,
take the books he read down from the shelf,
sort his letters, rearrange his clutter
to suit yourself.
You carry a box of paperbacks downstairs.
There on a pipe, the stranger you once were:
an old suit hanging in the cellar.

Waking

Dark nights in a ditch between two moons.
Then sky brightens. A searchlight sweeping over?
Like birds frightened out of sleep in low
catalpa trees, the past flutters awake;
it comes, a noisy trench of frogs in spring,
comes children playing out beyond the light
where the long dead pass evenings on the lawn,
great bobbing shadows taller than trees,
comes sudden chill discovery, as if you stepped,
hot, breathless, barefoot in the dark,
on brine and crushed ice spilled from the ice-
cream freezer, comes like the knock of huge
brindled moths bumping at the screen.

On the River Early

When fireflies plied lapping evening air
like jonboats the night river, and men laughed
under lanterns, loading gear, their massy
shadows giants climbing boathouse walls,
I lay in a lashed bed, dreams swimming slow
in the ring of light my yearning's mantle threw.

Is the river running backward into a time
thought gone forever? The morning's a smoky
lantern globe: off in the mist an outboard
motor sputters like yellow flame sucking
a charred wick dry. Voices rise, faint
on the river's glass. Long treeshadows climb
from the water talking, tall men coming home
whose breath I thought no longer fogged a mirror.

Sleepless

The prow runs grating up the gravel beach.
My boat rising under me, I step
down from a day and night on rocking water.
My feet remember nothing of the land:
the sandroad I am walking ripples, trees
tilt; from underfoot a toad leaps splashing
into grass. Schooled cattle rise and fall
in the wrinkled pasture lapping at barbed wire.

My cabin rides at anchor in the shade.
I bob in a fever of sleeplessness, all
I remember endlessly recurring: bullfrogs
karooming, water slap-slapping at
the bow. Pictures swim across the mind
like watersnakes through the ring of lantern light,
like fish rising from beneath a ledge,
gleaming in the sun, then flitting off.

Old ghost-face floating on the restless water,
are you momentum only of our days and nights
together, your voice a tossed relic, talk
that carries across a cove through morning fog?
Is my answer like a finger's twitch remembering
tapping on a line no longer held?

Berry Picking

I climb the sled road to the cattle bars
to shade so still I hear a soft bee-murmur.
Now wind streams through ash and white oak tops
like roaring of a far-off waterfall.
I have come to do my berry picking
by chestnut stumps once round as wagon wheels,
for berries grow sweeter here, and blacker, big
as my thumb about the mounds of rotting
richness ringed by briers, like graves untended.

This rusty plowfoot on a dumb rock pile
is no fit marker for your labor here.
I come to pick your fat blackberries
a moving monument who just this morning
tasted light new honey from your bees.

A Mountain Field

I hear the shower roaring down the ridge
and hurry to the mountain field's far edge.
A streaked column following the fence,
it crosses the sun, striking all at once,
buckshot all around me in the leaves.
It dances in the field like popping grease,
then passes down the mountain out of hearing.
I move out with the sun to berry briers.

Out of a startled sky lightning cracks,
sudden thunder rumbles at my back;
where I had taken cover from the shower,
a black horse, sleek and wet, stands staring.

I walk toward him holding out my hand;
he wheels, gallops along the fencerow,
cloud-shadow moving over the ground,
rises, clears the topmost strand and goes
a darting dragonfly through trees. All
night I hear him pawing in a stall.

Thaw

Onset: the eye of time begins to deepen.
Each moment leads you to a brink, a vista:
you walk cliffs above a frozen river.
At your back ruddy broomsage slithers
in warm wind blowing off green forever.

Woods stand open to the winter sun.
Along the ridge treeshadows scatter
black runes and crooked letters into coves.
Down the afternoon words fall and shatter,
icicles breaking up on river rocks.

In the night the river starts to move.
You lie listening to a deep wind neighing,

till morning drips at the eaves and you sit staring
at words written uphill in the dark.

Sowing Salt

This is a season of small miracles.
Dreamt from his rock by the barn, the fossil fish
swims in the light between barn roof and moon.
Scattered in the mountains, all my days
heave to their knees like cattle and come bawling
down from mountain pastures overnight,
starved for salt I sow over the rock.
I am restored. I salt the fish away.
Mother light licks me dry in a pasture.

Living Forever

1.

Sunday evening
three days since I slept.
My body aches, skin feels sore
like fever's onset.

Earth goes like a toy train on a track
into the dark tunnel
out again.
Others sleep wake sleep again
I will live forever.

2.

I grow sighted in the dark
take long walks
aware of a light behind the life
of stones. Their flesh glows
around a darkness, like fingers
held over the head of a flashlight—rosy
around the dark boneshadow.

3.

Like jointed rivercane a green house
shoots stories through clouds.
A yellow flower springs
from the mind's woodsdirt
growing toward lemon light.

The ground I stand on rolls,
a beast rising. I go
forward in a rocking boat, I walk
a soundless, sunlit ocean floor.
Weeds wave. A squid
goes flitting off, spreading
slow darkness.

Writing My Name

The letters of my signature tiptoe
like boys walking a tier pole in a barn.
Now the two *l*'s straddle it for fun,
skin a cat looping through themselves.

Is every signature a palimpsest,
a parchment page, today's text written
over a previous one imperfectly
removed? Are we such frugal monks?

Maybe our name's a creature born and born,
each metamorphosis recapitulating
all its former selves as it evolves.

Here beside an *r* sharp as a scorpion's
stinger—a fat larva loop, an *e*
soft and white as a grub, two *l*'s
tapered and delicate as wasp wings.

Once the letters crawled, a line of ants.
All orderly they marched erect, soldiers
behind their captains. They overcame kidstuff,
they loafed, did sudden handstands, slumped,

hung around, fellas scuffing the sidewalk
with their shoes. But if a spirit moved them,
they cut the figure wind traces in tall grass,
that water scrawls in sand as it is leaving.

Those names: you find them on the flyleaves
of old books, locust shells clinging
to dry bark.—But something is stirring here.

M's go humping along like those green worms
that measure you in summer for new clothes.
Each letter pauses, plays at being, imagines.

Two words certain only of becoming,
lazy on the page, like clouds—willing
weasels, whales, or foxes, as I please.

Planing Off

I lean into the tiller, the bow obeys.
Running straight for a drowned white oak
down channel, the buzzing outboard drives
wave wave wave of shudders
tense and singing through the boat.

I sit inside a rising falling drone
watching the shape of energy,
design symmetrical as a snowflake
danced out on water standing in the stern.
I cut the throttle back, the figure melts;
it comes again with power.

The drowned white oak comes running
at the prow. I cut a rolling arc
around those standing bones.
Planing off, running for Round Island,
I am become an energy's anatomy, force
fleshed out to form—until a power lays
within me, like wind, or wanders on,
leaving shape of itself
in my settled sand.

Driving to the Gulf

Behind the hill headlights come
sliding yellow on swung bellies
of power lines. Between kudzu banks
reaching for each other, the beams
touch down and run past, wings flapping.

Over the hill another town
glows like a jar of fireflies
boys called in to bed leave on the lawn.
Just as I enter, at the hour
of "Life Line," "The World Tomorrow,"
all the traffic lights start blinking caution.

Stations overlap
all up and down the band.
Behind "The Star Spangled Banner"
and Radio Cuba, wandering in
and out, a Strauss waltz
turns like a lost brook.
A country of blue mountains
and fast-falling creeks, rocky gorges,

I tilt into piney flats, swamps
spooked by spanish moss.
My breathing rushes and runs back,
eddies around hilltop tobacco barns.
On silent beaches of my breath
gulls cry, circling
drowning mountain pastures.

On Native Ground

This wind is blowing me all time's weathers,
mingling near and far, pennyrile
and woodsmoke, crow's call and carrion.
In a jay's harangue saws are singing; the swung
ax flashes in a lifting wave; twanging
still in a white-faced hornet's whine
a barbed-wire fence caught in a cuff once crossing.

Seed fallen in flesh rich as woodsdirt,
gone days spring up, trees from sown sweat.
Now is this green tree's growing bark, this always
was and is and forever tree-shading
summer was and is and summer will be.

A waterbead quivers on my hand:
there is a way to enter. Underfoot
a mole's nightwork gives way—O doors
are everywhere: the spring at the mountain's
foot holds the running taste of childhood,
the barking fox blurts the mountain's riddle.
Transparent minnows hanging in green water:
windows onto sunken summer days.
I enter through a fish's eye to one
vast room glowing in cold light.
Out of an oilspill on a rainslick road
campfires of a hundred hunts are blazing.
A dog's eye caught in headlights on a turn:

rose windows warm in his cathedral skull.
I travel everywhere on native ground;
roads turning into darkness turn me home,
plunge me into cool air of the mountains.

Gray marble monuments bending in a graveyard,
skewed reflections swaying on rolled water,
straighten to still gray chestnut stumps,
a chimney stack among old trees and roses
sprawling over tumbled corner stones
sprouting second growth. A new house rises.
Life grows in rings around a hurt,
a tree with barbed wire running through its heart.

PART THREE: *FAMILY REUNION*

County Seat

Turtles on a log,
old men sit sunning
on a bench in front of the courthouse.
They have been talking of old times
while the clock tower's shadow,
like a black cat stalking field mice,
has inched forward
somehow without ever moving.

Visit to an Ancient Lady

1.

Once you were a sibyl Sunday mornings in that parlor
where bearded forbears
gazed from ovals on the blistered walls.
Kindled on camphor, transcendent on simples
from your window sill, a woolen wrap
against the sabbath chill,
you read the needlework in your lap,
prophesied the plunder of your eyes
and pictured George a wolf in overalls,
bullet-fingered George who farmed for shares
and fleeced only the simple sheep. . . .

2.

But not even sibyls, hoary-haired and wise,
find footing where their hard-shelled oracles
flit backward through deceptive deep
like crawfish in a pool.
For while you quilted clues
and pieced together a George with teeth and claws,
a shiftier tenant pulled a subtler wool:—
took your house and land in kind, stole you blind,
reduced you to this rented room and bed
where you lie, landless now, your great white head
how rapt, for you must grope to thread
the needle's eye.

3.

That broad-backed brute who seemed to know his place,
who seemed content with shares, is proved a rogue.
Prowling that house, the mind, pilfering there,
he sullies a shambles of verses, broken faces,
and declamation pieces beneath his brogues.
Listening in the dark,
you sense the nearness of that burly man.
His coming is the arc this swinging fan
draws sickle-shaped and cool across your face.

Miss Hattie Mae, Aged 92,
Dies at the Quality Extended Care Facility

Tree roots are snapping underground.
Black woodsdirt tumbling in her mouth

tastes like rain. A wart-faced gnome
peers out, then pulls a hole in after him.

The startled owl clicks his beak and flies
through a pane of glass.

Jagged planes,
angles shatter on a screen that drones.

Eyes float on water and blue eels
wave and wave on swaying mirrored hills.

Up through leaves like listening ears a path leads.
There:—a rose-red plain and pyramids.

Howard Lays His Burden Down at Last

He pulled each day on like a shoe a size
too small, and though it plagued and pinched, he wore it
for the future's sake. He moved through
the planned rows of his life waging war
with fire and chemicals on beetles, mites
and moles, starlings and thistles—every varmint
out to eat his farm from under him.
All his tomorrows were a load he carried.
He couldn't set them down, not even when
in dreams scarecrows holding onto their hats
fled watermelon patches for the dole
and thick-lipped horses raped his freckled daughters.

Aunt Gladys's Home Movie #31 (Albert's Funeral)

Narration: Aunt Dessie, Eunice, Cora, Frankie, Gladys,
        Uncle Martin, Hubert, Charles, Bestrum.
Sound: Music from "Gunsmoke" in the tv room where the
    children are.

Our chairs drawn to one end of the living
room, we sit like faithful at a Sunday evening
service, viewing a miracle. Before our eyes
Albert stirs in the ticking coil of dark
film and comes riding a beam of light,
a smear of colors, finger painting—flowers.

Focus it better, Martin. It's flowers. Flowers
in Albert's garden. Not another living
soul loved flowers like Albert. Look how the light
falls over those. Must've been late in the evening.
La, la, that's pretty! What do you call that dark
red one, Glad? If that's not a sight for sore eyes!

Santa! It's Albert. The boys can't believe their eyes.
There they are, Glad. Poinsettias. Christmas flowers,
we always called them. What's that one? bloomed in the dark
in the cellar after Albert gave it up ever living.
Like four o'clocks. They don't open till the evening
shade hits em, won't open in bright light.

You took that, Glad.—Bestrum, you're in my light.
Albert caught one! Look at the boys—eyes
big as saucers! The ocean's pretty in the evening

like that. Charleston Gardens. With all those flowers
I bet Albert just thought of going and living
there. That's laurel on the parkway, it was too dark—
But if it had a bloom, it was never too dark
for Albert. He always used to make light
of his movies. I always said he could make a living
taking pictures. They say some men's eyes
got dollar signs in 'em. Albert had flowers
in his. He was in that garden every evening

after supper. He was in it morning *and* evening.
There it is. The boys—so grown-up in their dark
suits. That wreath—made from some of the flowers
he grew. They don't show up good here, the light
under the tent's too dim. But I never laid eyes
on prettier flowers at a funeral in all my living

days. Lights, somebody! You know those evening flowers
that open in the dark—Well, now, Glad, dry your eyes,
honey. You have to close your mind and go on living!

Martin Gets Away

He lies beached, drowning in dry air.
Nurses pass and pass like screaming gulls.
Backed into a dark place in his lung,
deep as a festering hook, sits a crab.
Arms are working crablike over him;
busy scissor-claws and hot eye-beams
hoist him toward a mouth,—but now seawater
rises in him throbbing, lifts him free.
Righting himself, he slips through clumsy arms
and goes, glides, trailing tubes like broken
lines gone slack, off into the dark
effortless perfection of a dream.
Arms are treading water overhead,
gull shadows swoop soundlessly and pass.

My Uncle's Death Alters the Course of History

I am watching Aunt Eunice and remembering
the Cuban missile crisis
when Sara, near hysteria, called
all the way from London
and found her mother vague about it all.
"I let your father take care of things like that."

What will she do now
if we have a recession, or if
the basement floods, or the Russians
act up again, or the Democrats?
Martin always took care of things like that.

She sits cleaning her glasses
with a tissue, seeing no one.
We are all murmurs, bobbing blurs
of great world issues.

Remembering Wade Robinson

Wade comes unsolicited
out of my twelfth year
like a renewal offer from *Boys' Life*
or catalogs for Daisy air rifles
my mother dutifully forwards.
There is a hissing, the mind turns
a field of broomsage running under wind.
Wade is standing there—
perhaps since I last remembered—
in faded denims, black hat,
like a dog winding snow-sky,
or a mule head-down in a pasture corner,
gray, motionless as a fencepost
but following through all the address changes,
always about to tell me something.

After we stood in week-old snow
outside his house, calling, calling
(it was my uncle who stomped
onto the boarded-up porch, entered,
and found Wade frozen clothes on the floor),
I saw the shoebox full of his drawings,
hundreds of schemes on lined tablet paper:
perspectives of telephone poles marching
overland, atop each pole a saucer
catching broken-line rays of the sun;
an airplane with wings that flapped.

This gray snow-sky and bleak field
framed in the window conjure
Wade Robinson, I tell myself.
I sit picturing nieces and nephews,
their child-faces mounted on grown-up
bodies, sifting through shoeboxes
of my poems, shaking their heads, laughing.
The sky lowers over the field like a sheet;
sparse second-growth is stubble
sprouted on a corpse's face.

Craig Speaks

1.

It was early June. Out in the yard an army
of horned green worms, black stripes down their backs,
marched up our two catalpa trees to eat
our afternoon shade. "Oh, well," Mom said, passing
new potatoes boiled in their jackets, passing
leaf lettuce wilted under bacon grease,
"the Lord giveth and the Lord taketh away."
"The worms always show up in early June,"
Dad said. "Never fail."
                                        A loss suffered
every year, and right on time, made sense.

O when they feather-dusted blessings and burdens
like bookends holding up a shelf of wisdom,
or said, "Look here, the thing works this way,
so that's what it is,"—it was as if
something lived in the house they still denied,—
an idiot child locked in a room upstairs
playing with streaks of sunlight like a cat.

2.

The news drove up crisply uniformed. A moan—
at first it came from nowhere—a moan born
a cat's meow grew to a bawling calf
and died, still nothing human, shuddering.
My mother's body shook. She heard the news:
my brother is coming home, and since a mine
exploded him, he will arrive from Saigon
pieces of a puzzle in a box.

3.

I won't reassemble him someone
he never was, a picture for the blind.
Had he come home even half whole, I know
he'd have roared his manhood out through twin exhausts
and laid burnt rubber down on all the roads.
Brown-eyed cows bedded in fence-corners
near the road would have crashed cattle bars,
leaped four-strand fences bellowing and gone
dry when he tore thunder, smoke, and sparks
around a turn. Girls all summer long
would have awakened pale and deeply sore.

My father's head turns in his bent arm
resting against the wall. "It don't make sense."
Before he's done it will, because it must.
My brother's myth stirs bleating toward its birth.

4.

I have lived with senselessness a year.
It came to live upstairs in his room
the day my brother went off to this war.
It has grown from grief into a daily chore,
a hulking idiot child with sparse horse hair
and runny eyes in a swollen pumpkin head.

I hear it moving crablike over the floor
foraging on its own excrement.

A Soldier

Black fenceposts pitch and stagger down the ridge
like comrades bearing him home from that patrol.

In this farmhouse on Newfound Creek
he is a uniform, a framed grin
looking down from the mantlepiece.

A porch swing creaking, creaking helps
treefrogs sing the evening greener, drowning
the light in his retouched eyes.

A clock ticks, clock ticks.
In the dark a back door opens, letting
a streak of yellow light out like a cat.

We are beginning to believe his death
as the rosiness of his cheeks
becomes the undertaker's cosmetology.

Aunt Vi

After we found the love letters
in the barn, among straw
and tobacco sticks, in shoeboxes
muddaubers had built on—
envelopes with Pvt.,
Cpl., Sgt.—
on a July afternoon
when the hot tin roof popped and cracked
the code of S. W. A. K.,

Aunt Vi never aged beyond
her photographs in the album.
We read between the lines
of her weathered face,
studied her faded blue eyes,
interpreted the freckles
on the back of her hand,
the white spots
under her fingernails.

The Bee Woman

She carried the eggs in her straw hat and never
reached into a nest with her bare hand.
A woman who could conjure warts, who knew
charms for drawing fire, spells to make
butter come, and mysteries of bees
and hummingbirds, besides, knew to roll
eggs from a guinea's nest with a gooseneck hoe.

There is a mountain cove and light is leaving.
Speckled guineas fly to roost in trees,
their potterick and screech drifts far away,
becomes the faintest peeping in my dream
of stifling afternoons when we would stand,
the old woman and I, by fencerows and cowtrails
listening for half-wild guineas screeching
as they came off nests they'd stolen away
in thickets, briers, scrub pines, and chinquapins.

And no matter where I wake—horn's beep,
ship's bells, clatter of garbage cans,
strange tongues spoken on the street below,
in a rising falling bunk out at sea,—
everywhere I stand on native ground.
The bee woman may pass through my dream:
running under a cloud of swarming bees,
she beats an empty pie pan with a spoon
till the swarm settles, black on a drooping pine bough
and guineas regroup potterricking—all
moving toward waking's waterfall.

Visitors

Like relatives coming south in summer
to make a week of Sundays in the house,
they kept arriving
in dreams of car doors slamming in the night.

Now they people this vision.
I'm walking with them through remembered rooms.

It is no wonder the dead come visiting
this morning. After last night's storm the air
is so clear, even the mountains
have moved closer.

Family Reunion

Sunlight glints off the chrome of many cars.
Cousins chatter like a flock of guineas.

In the shade of oaks and maples
six tables stand
filled with good things to eat.
Only the jars of iced tea sweat.

Here the living and dead mingle
like sun and shadow under old trees.

For the dead have come too,
those dark, stern departed who pose
all year in oval picture frames.

They are looking out of the eyes of children,
young sprouts
whose laughter blooms
fresh as the new flowers in the graveyard.